TINY BATTLEFIELDS

FIGHTING MALARIA

ROBYN HARDYMAN

Gareth Stevens
PUBLISHING

Please visit our website, www.garethstevens.com. For a free color catalog of all our high-quality books, call toll free 1-800-542-2595 or fax 1-877-542-2596.

Hardyman, Robyn.
Fighting malaria / by Robyn Hardyman.
p. cm. -- (Tiny battlefields)
Includes index.
ISBN 978-1-4824-1347-2 (pbk.)
ISBN 978-1-4824-1310-6 (6-pack)
ISBN 978-1-4824-1454-7 (library binding)
1. Malaria -- Juvenile literature. I. Hardyman, Robyn. II. Title.
RA644.M2 H37 2015
616.9--d23

Library of Congress Cataloging-in-Publication Data

First Edition

Published in 2015 by
Gareth Stevens Publishing
111 East 14th Street, Suite 349
New York, NY 10003

© 2015 Gareth Stevens Publishing

Produced by: Calcium, www.calciumcreative.co.uk
Designed by: Simon Borrough
Edited by: Sarah Eason and Jennifer Sanderson
Picture research by: Rachel Blount

Photo credits: Cover: Shutterstock: Raj Creationzs; Inside: Centers for Disease Control and Prevention: James Gathany 15, 24, Gary Meek 41, Dr. Mae Melvin 26; Dreamstime: Mr.Smith Chetanachan 17, Dimaberkut 8, Matt Fowler 9, Alan Gignoux 38, Kelvintt 36, Albert Komlos 20, Alexandr Mitiuc 6, Molekuul 28, Samrat35 22, Smandy 23, Birute Vijeikiene 19; Flickr: NIAID 3, 14, The U.S. Food and Drug Administration 30, 31, U.S. Army Africa, Rick Scavetta 35, 40, 43; Malaria No More: 32, Geoff Ward 33; Shutterstock: 360b 45, Hector Conesa 44, Garsya 25, GuoZhongHua 29, Ian MacLellan 37, Mrfiza 27, 39, RAJ CREATIONZS 1, Pal Teravagimov 34; The Global Fund: John Rae 5, 10, 18; Wikimedia Commons: Mike Blyth 12, Jim Gathany/CDC 4, Andy Mettler/World Economic Forum 13, Nephron 42, Oxfam East Africa 16, Bjørn Christian Tørrissen 21, U.S. National Archives and Records Administration 7, Desmond Utomwen 11.

Printed in the United States of America

CPSIA compliance information: Batch #CS15GS: For further information contact Gareth Stevens, New York, New York at 1-800-542-2595.

CONTENTS

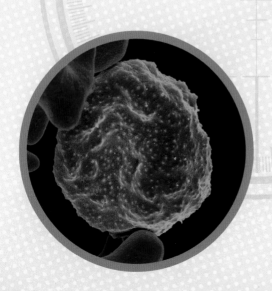

CHAPTER 1: WAGING WAR

The battle against disease is as old as human history. It is only in the last 100 years, however, that people have begun to arm themselves with effective weapons for the fight. Today, science and medicine are waging a complex and sophisticated global war. One of the most challenging targets is against the tiny parasite that causes malaria.

What Is Malaria?

Malaria is an infectious disease. It can be easily passed from one person to another. Minute microorganisms called pathogens cause infectious diseases. There are three types of pathogens: virus, bacterium, and protozoon, or parasite. Protozoa are single-celled, like bacteria, but larger, and are often spread by insects. Malaria is caused by parasites called plasmodiums and is spread by the bite of female anopheles mosquitoes. These mosquitoes breed in water and multiply quickly.

Deadly Bite

The mosquito's saliva contains plasmodiums, which enter a person's blood when he or she is bitten by the mosquito.

When a female anopheles mosquito bites a person, the malaria plasmodiums in its saliva enter the person's bloodstream.

Plasmodiums travel to the liver, where they reproduce. They then flood out of the liver and back into the blood vessels, making some red blood cells burst and causing a fever. The most serious type of malaria is caused by plasmodium falciparum. This type of malaria must be treated differently from the other most common type, plasmodium vivax. This strain makes the red blood cells stick together and block the blood vessels, which deprives the body of oxygen.

Malaria causes enormous suffering and usually has the worst impact among children.

Signs and Symptoms

The symptoms of malaria can take up to one month to surface after a mosquito bite. Malaria causes fever, weakness, vomiting, and fits that cause the patient to shake violently. Difficulty breathing can also be a symptom. Without treatment, patients often die, especially if they are children. People who survive often experience a return of their symptoms over the years. Malaria is one of the leading causes of death around the world. The disease is responsible for up to 1 million deaths each year.

"A child now dies every minute from malaria, and that is one child and one minute too many."

Ray Chambers, the UN Secretary-General's Special Envoy for Malaria

Who Is at Risk?

Malaria is a very widespread disease. Almost half of the world's population is at risk of catching it—that is 3.3 billion people living in 109 countries. Malaria kills up to 1 million people every year, and most of these are women and children.

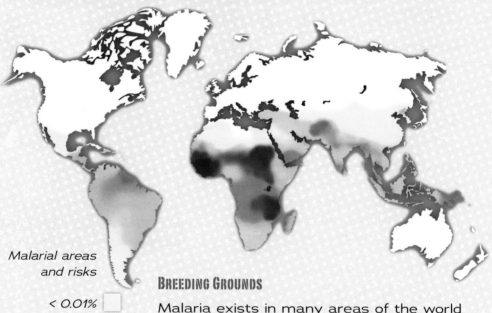

Malarial areas and risks

< 0.01%	
0.01–0.1%	
0.1–1%	
1–10%	
10–25%	
>24%	

This map shows the areas of the world with the highest rates of malaria. It is very clear that malaria is particularly severe in sub-Saharan Africa.

Breeding Grounds

Malaria exists in many areas of the world where the climate is warm and humid because this creates the best breeding conditions for anopheles mosquitoes. Malaria tends to be found in the tropics, Asia, the Americas, and Africa. The huge majority of malaria cases occur in sub-Saharan Africa. The World Health Organization (WHO) has estimated that in 2010 there were 219 million documented cases of malaria. That year, the disease killed between 660,000 and 1.2 million people, many of whom were children in Africa. The actual number of deaths is not known with certainty because accurate data is unavailable in many rural areas and many cases are undocumented.

PERMANENTLY PRESENT

Malaria is endemic in several countries. This means that it never goes away, unlike other infectious diseases such as influenza, or the flu, or cholera. Endemic diseases strike from time to time in epidemics or, on a larger scale, as pandemics.

TOURISTS AND TRAVELERS

Visitors to affected areas are at risk of catching malaria. More and more people are traveling to malarial areas as tourists or for business. They may return from a trip and only begin to feel sick a few weeks later. This is because it can take up to one month for the plasmodium to break out of the liver. It is just as important for people traveling to a country with a malaria problem to take preventive measures as it is for everyone living in malarial areas.

"I just started to sweat so hard my head began pounding ... I went to the hospital and they diagnosed me pretty immediately with malaria. I had a temperature of over 104°F (40°C) and was unable to move or leave my bed for two weeks..."

Andrew Wylde, a 24-year-old traveler to Ghana in West Africa who contracted malaria

This poster was produced during World War II to warn military personnel in malaria-infected areas to protect themselves against the disease.

DON'T GO TO BED WITH A MALARIA MOSQUITO

★ SLEEP UNDER A NET! ★ KEEP IT REPAIRED! ★ TUCK IT IN! ★

BE SURE NO MOSQUITO IS INSIDE WAITING FOR YOU

FIGHT THE PERIL BEHIND THE LINES

A Cycle of Poverty

Malaria causes untold misery to millions of people each year. Its effect not only makes people sick, but also threatens the economic progress of much of the developing world.

Children in developing countries must stay well and go to school to have the best chance to improve their living standards.

The Cost to Society

Malaria has a devastating effect on countries where it is endemic. Sick and dying children are deprived of opportunities for education and a chance to improve their lives. Adults who are sick with malaria cannot work. Their families depend on their ability to grow food or to provide money from a job. Without food or an income, families cannot raise themselves out of poverty. As long as they are in poverty, people are also more likely to get sick. Malaria is estimated to cost Africa more than $12 billion dollars a year in direct costs such as health care and in lost economic activity.

LIVING STANDARDS

The battle against malaria includes the fight to improve the living standards of people in affected countries. When people do not have enough to eat or they have to work all the time just to survive, their immune systems become weaker and they are less able to fight off disease. The health systems in affected countries are often poorly developed so people cannot easily gain access to medical care. Parents may walk for several days with a sick child to reach a clinic for medical treatment. Even when drugs and other treatments can be found, they are often too expensive for many people to buy.

TACKLING POVERTY

Solving the problems of poverty is very complicated, but an enormous amount is being done. Governments and many other agencies around the world are investing in measures to improve living standards and access to medical care. They hope that, when malaria strikes, people are in a stronger position to fight back.

At this clinic in southern Sudan, Africa, a doctor has many patients to see and far fewer resources than most doctors in the developed world.

"The reality is straightforward. The power of existing interventions is not matched by the power of health systems to deliver them to those in greatest need, in a comprehensive way, and on an adequate scale."

Margaret Chan, director general of WHO

CHAPTER 2: A GLOBAL BATTLE

Malaria is a problem for the whole world even if most people who catch the disease live in developing countries. It is closely linked with the even bigger issues facing the world today—poverty and inequality. These issues cause many of the situations that worsen the outbreak and spread of malaria. The good news is that the knowledge and tools to dramatically reduce malaria worldwide already exist. The challenge is to use them more effectively.

Distributing preventive measures to the people who need them is an important part of the global effort against malaria.

THE SUCCESS AND FAILINGS OF 1955

In 1955, a global push to eradicate malaria was launched. It had some success, eliminating the disease in many wealthy countries and reducing it elsewhere. However, it faltered and failed when the political commitment and the funding came to an end. As a result, malaria roared back across Africa and parts of Asia and South America.

MILLENNIUM DECLARATION

In September 2000, world leaders came together at the United Nations (UN) in New York City to adopt the United Nations Millennium Declaration. This committed their members to a new global partnership to reduce extreme poverty. It set out a series of time-bound targets— with a deadline of 2015—known as the eight Millennium Development Goals (MDGs). The goals are focused on improvements in health, wealth, and education. It is hoped they will halt and begin to reverse the incidence of malaria and other major diseases by 2015.

ROLL BACK MALARIA

The Roll Back Malaria Partnership is the global framework for implementing coordinated action against the disease. It includes more than 500 partners including governments, businesses, charities, and research institutions. The great strength of Roll Back Malaria lies in its ability to form effective partnerships both globally and nationally. Partners work together to scale up malaria-control efforts at country level, ensuring they make the best use of resources.

"We are making significant and durable progress in battling a major public health problem ... But there are worrisome signs that suggest progress might slow."

WHO, World Malaria Report, 2011

Precious Kalamba Gbeneol is a doctor and the special assistant to the president of Nigeria on Millennium Development Goals. She is in charge of the country's $1 billion budget to achieve the goals in her country.

One Step At A Time

The Roll Back Malaria Partnership has outlined two phases in the fight against malaria. In the short and medium term, people need to use their existing knowledge to treat those suffering from the disease and prevent it from spreading. In the longer term, the goal is to eliminate malaria altogether. This would be a truly extraordinary achievement.

This is the intensive care unit for children in a hospital in Nigeria. The children are sleeping under bed nets to protect them from mosquito bites.

Meeting Challenges

The immediate aim is that by 2015 the MDG should be achieved so that malaria is no longer a major cause of death anywhere in the world. It should therefore also not be a barrier to social and economic development and growth in countries where it used to be at extremely high levels. By 2015, levels of malaria worldwide should have fallen by 75 percent compared with the year 2000. Beyond 2015, it will be essential for everyone involved to keep up their commitment, or there is a real risk that malaria levels will rise again as a global threat. The return of malaria after the end of the campaign of the 1950s illustrates the importance of this.

Eradicating Malaria

If the MDG aims can be achieved, and it is a big "if," there is a possibility of eradicating malaria for good. Only at that point can efforts to control the disease be stepped down. Some partners in the fight against malaria are focused on this long-term goal. Others are working on the immediate crisis to treat today's patients, prevent malaria's spread, and ensure that at least 80 percent of people at risk have access to these services.

"I'd be disappointed if within 20 years we're not very close to eradicating this globally."

Bill Gates at the Bill and Melinda Gates Foundation Forum in Seattle in 2011

At the World Economic Forum in Davos, Switzerland, in 2008, Bill Gates (second from right) called for businesses, governments, and nonprofit organizations to work together more effectively to combat the threat of diseases such as malaria.

ATTACK ON TWO FRONTS

Any fight against disease has two main areas of focus: prevention and treatment. Both of these are vital parts of the strategy in the first phase of the battle against malaria.

Vaccination could prevent the malaria plasmodium (right) from affecting a person's blood.

PREVENTION

Scientists all over the world are working to find new ways to combat the threat of malaria. Some of their work is in the area of prevention. They are looking for new ways to kill mosquitoes or to prevent them from passing on the infection. Other scientists are looking at better ways to diagnose malaria. New medication is also being developed all the time. Perhaps the area with the greatest potential for the future is the search for a malaria vaccine, which could be the most powerful preventive weapon of all.

CONTROLLING MALARIA

In the United States, the Centers for Disease Control and Prevention (CDC) began in 1946 as an agency to control malaria in the United States. Malaria is no longer widespread in the United States, but the CDC continues to provide leadership and expertise in global malaria-control activities. New medicines, diagnostic tests, and mosquito control products may soon be available, and the CDC has begun to develop effective strategies for using and evaluating them.

Educating the World

In countries where malaria is common, education programs teach people about the dangers of stagnant water where mosquitoes breed. They also teach about the importance of using preventive measures. Every year, April 25 is World Malaria Day. This is a time to focus people's attention on the cause and to celebrate what has been achieved. It also shines a light on the latest innovations and encourages individuals, institutions, and governments to contribute to the funding of vital work.

The CDC in the United States provides both leadership and expertise in the global fight against malaria.

15

Chapter 3: Preventing Malaria

To prevent malaria, the work must be done on the ground where the disease is at its height. It is essential to provide the equipment and technology to prevent people catching malaria and to make sure that it is put to use.

New Technology

Scientists around the world are working on new preventive technologies in several areas. Some of these technologies are focused on the mosquitoes and are designed to kill them in their breeding grounds and in people's homes. They also work to prevent the mosquitoes from making contact with people. Other scientists are focused on the people who are at risk.

They are developing medication to protect the most vulnerable from catching malaria. At the moment, there is no vaccine against malaria, but there is a massive global effort underway to develop one. A breakthrough would be a huge step forward.

Stagnant water provides a fertile breeding ground for malaria-carrying mosquitoes. The clearing of these drainage ditches is an effective preventive measure.

STAYING AHEAD

Together, all the measures against malaria are saving millions of lives worldwide. The situation is constantly changing, however. The mosquitoes may respond to preventive measures by developing resistance to insecticides or medication, so the battle must be constantly pushed forward in the laboratory and on the ground. Science must stay one step ahead, with new innovations all the time.

ANTIMALARIAL DRUGS

Travelers to malarial countries can take medication to protect themselves. There are several different drugs available. These drugs work only for a limited period, which is why they are not suitable for people living in malarial areas. They are also limited because mosquitoes develop resistance to the drugs. For example, chloroquine and paludrine are generally taken together, but they are beginning to lose their efficacy in Africa. Another drug, lariam, is no longer effective in Southeast Asia. Travelers must take the correct medication suited to their destination.

Mosquito larvae will hatch out of these pupae in the water.

On the Battlefield

Antimalarial drugs must often be taken for a period of time before traveling to a malarial area and for a time after the traveler's return. The CDC publishes a table showing every country's level of risk, type of malaria, most suitable medication to take, and any known drug resistance. This is all essential safety information for travelers.

LIFESAVING MOSQUITO NETS

The first line of defense against malaria is to sleep beneath a net. The nets form a barrier to mosquitoes and, because they are treated with insecticide, will kill them. One net is needed for every two people. That means that 730 million nets are needed globally, and 250 million of those are needed in Africa.

BUYING THE NETS

The mosquitoes that carry malaria are most active at night, so sleeping under antimalarial nets offers excellent protection against the insects' bites. The nets are relatively cheap. Hundreds of millions of them have been distributed to countries affected by malaria, and this work is continuing. A recent innovation has been to arrange for the nets to be bought in enormous quantities. Centralizing the purchase of nets saves a lot of money, which can then be spent on other measures.

Simple nets, such as this one, are saving lives around the world.

By 2014, the Global Fund, the world's largest financier of antimalarial programs, bulk-bought 190 million nets, saving $140 million. This bulk purchase also ensured there is a regular supply of nets.

The Global Fund is also supporting moves toward the manufacturing of the nets in countries where there is a high demand for them. This delivers many benefits including lower transportation costs and advice from local experts.

The Downside to Nets

There are some problems with mosquito nets. They wear out and must be replaced. The nets develop holes and repeated washing removes the insecticide. New research is focused on the durability of the net fabric and the insecticides. The prolonged exposure to insecticides can cause health problems among some people, and, furthermore, the mosquitoes can develop resistance to the insecticide.

A New Kind of Fabric

One new technology scientists are focusing on is developing a net fabric that physically damages the mosquitoes when they touch it. They are then prevented from feeding and so die soon after. No insecticide is involved, so the net is harmless to humans. Research is also continuing into new, more effective insecticides.

On the Battlefield

In the first half of 2013, 30 million insecticide-treated nets were distributed under programs supported by the Global Fund, taking the total number of nets distributed to 340 million.

Several innovative new technologies are being developed to improve the durability and effectiveness of mosquito nets.

SPRAYING

Airplanes fly low over areas where mosquitoes breed, spraying them with insecticide.

Insecticides are also used to kill mosquitoes in other ways. They can be sprayed onto the inside walls of homes to kill the insects when they land there. About 172 million households need to be sprayed every year. Insecticide can also be sprayed outdoors over the areas where mosquitoes breed and live. This is known as vector control.

WALL-TO-WALL INSECTICIDE

Long-lasting chemical insecticides are sprayed on the walls of people's homes in malarial areas. When the mosquitoes come inside in the evening, they are killed on impact. Spraying is time-consuming and lasts for only a few months, so other options are being researched. The CDC is supporting research into the use of durable insecticide wall liners in an area of western Kenya. In 2010, wall liners were installed in 1,700 homes. The preliminary analysis suggests that new malaria infections fell by 38 percent as a result of the liners. The homes are being monitored every six months to see how effective the liners remain.

INSECTICIDE-FREE PAINT

Another recent area of research is developing a paint coating that kills the mosquitoes without insecticide. The paint contains natural minerals that kill the insects when they touch it. The paint removes the protective layer that covers their bodies, making the mosquito dry up and die. It works on many kinds of insects and has no ill effects on humans.

VECTOR CONTROL

Outdoors, vector control is practiced by spraying insecticide over stagnant water areas where mosquitoes breed. This can kill a large number of insects at once, but it is difficult to eliminate all breeding grounds effectively. Vector control remains a useful preventive measure when used with other weapons in the ongoing battle against malaria.

On the Battlefield

Another method of vector control is to catch the mosquitoes in traps. One new research project is developing traps that contain synthetic odors that mimic the odor of humans to attract female mosquitoes. Once the mosquitoes enter the trap, an insecticide kills them and a larvicide kills any larvae that hatch from their eggs. The device is powered by solar panels and needs only to have water added to it to make it active. This makes it ideal for remote areas.

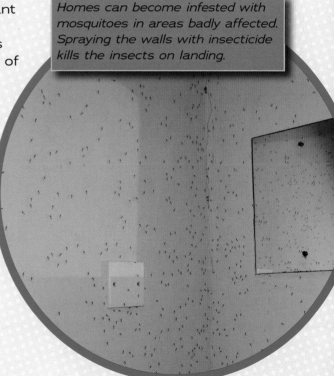

Homes can become infested with mosquitoes in areas badly affected. Spraying the walls with insecticide kills the insects on landing.

Protection During Pregnancy

Pregnant women are at increased risk of contracting malaria. When they do catch it, they are more likely to die than other people with the disease. This high-risk group is a particular target for preventive measures.

Affecting the Unborn Child

Malaria in pregnant women is particularly serious because the unborn child is likely to be affected. Malaria in pregnancy causes stillbirths and babies with low birth weight. The babies are also more likely to die in their first year. The most serious kind of malaria, plasmodium falciparum, is especially dangerous during pregnancy, but the second most common kind, plasmodium vivax, can also affect the unborn child.

Prevention and Control

The Roll Back Malaria Partnership and WHO recommend that every pregnant woman in a high-risk area receive at least two doses of an antimalarial drug during her pregnancy. This means that about 25 million women in Africa alone need this treatment every year. It has been shown to be remarkably effective, dramatically improving the chances of pregnant women remaining healthy. Roll Back Malaria has a

Protecting pregnant women from malaria is an important preventive measure for individuals and their communities.

Women receive education about the importance of having antimalarial treatment during pregnancy, to protect both themselves and their babies.

Malaria in Pregnancy Working Group to provide strategic advice on the best practices for the prevention and control of malaria during pregnancy.

MALARIA IN PREGNANCY CONSORTIUM

The Malaria in Pregnancy Consortium exists to improve the control of malaria in pregnancy in Africa, Asia, and Latin America. It includes 47 partner institutions in 32 countries. As part of its work, it is evaluating at least one safe and effective alternative to the current medication given to pregnant women, sulphadoxine-pyrimethamine, because resistance to this drug is increasing in some areas.

"The overall goal of the project is not only to develop new antimalaria in pregnancy prevention but also to promote European and African research collaboration and strengthen the capacity of African institutions to conduct clinical research."

The Malaria in Pregnancy Consortium

23

CHAPTER 4: TREATING MALARIA

Malaria is a treatable disease. A few dollars will pay for a course of treatment that can save the life of an infected child in just a few days. However, malaria has persisted for centuries because it adapts to changing circumstances and develops resistance to antimalarial drugs and also to pesticides. It also resurges whenever action against it slows. New research into treatments is needed all the time to fight malaria.

DIFFERENT KINDS OF DRUG

There are several types of drugs to treat the different kinds of malaria. For many years, chloroquine was commonly used against falciparum malaria but, because the parasite developed widespread resistance to it, it is rarely used as a treatment today. Scientists have now developed new, more effective drugs to replace chloroquine.

Drug companies around the world are testing new treatments in the hope of finding more effective antimalarial medication.

TREATING LATE-STAGE MALARIA

There are many issues that affect the successful use of treatment drugs on the ground. In many African countries, small and remote village communities have little or no health care. Parents often walk for days with their sick children to find a doctor. It is much more difficult to treat malaria when it is at a late stage, but this is one target for the latest research. Several new drugs are in the pipeline for late-stage malaria.

Just one dollar can save the life of a child with malaria by paying for a course of treatment.

STORING THE DRUGS

Once antimalarial drugs have been distributed, they must be kept in the correct conditions to stay active. Many drugs currently in use have a shelf life of up to only two years. This can be difficult in the developing world. One new drug in the pipeline is addressing this problem and should have a shelf life of at least three years.

"The distribution of lifesaving drugs has been a total lifesaving, game-changing event for so many families and their children ... A treatment costs only one dollar to buy and deliver to a child."

Hillary Clinton

DIAGNOSING DISEASE

Diagnosis is always the first step in any treatment plan. There are several reasons why it is so important for medical professionals to be able to diagnose malaria both quickly and accurately.

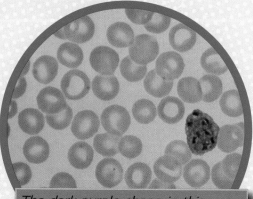

The dark purple shape in this image is malaria plasmodium inside an infected red blood cell.

IS IT MALARIA?

Doctors must know whether or not a patient is suffering from malaria because there are other diseases that cause similar symptoms. If it is malaria, it is vital to know which kind of malaria it is because the drug treatments are different for each one. Crucially, the drugs used to treat malaria work best when the disease is in the early stages. It is just as important to know if the patient is, in fact, not suffering from malaria. Antimalarial drugs need not then be wasted. This saves money and it also brings another benefit: the more the drugs are used, the greater the chances of the mosquitoes developing resistance to them.

RAPID DIAGNOSTIC TESTS

In the past, malaria was diagnosed by examining a blood sample under a microscope. This takes time and is not practical in remote areas. In recent years, huge progress has been made with creating and distributing Rapid Diagnostic Tests (RDTs). These enable health workers to diagnose malaria from a pinprick of blood. They do not need expensive equipment, and the results are known in minutes. In 2005, about 200,000 RDTs were distributed to malaria-endemic countries. By 2009, this figure was 33 million and, by 2010, it was 88 million. The testing rate in the public sector in WHO's African Region rose from 20 percent in 2005 to 45 percent in 2010.

TESTING IN KENYA

The Kenyan government has adopted a policy of testing everyone with a fever before giving them treatment. International funding bodies gave the Kenyan government 1.7 million RDTs and supported the training of health workers to use them. Children brought to clinics are now tested immediately and, if necessary, start treatment within minutes, rather than hours or days.

"Malaria RDTs have helped ease congestion in the laboratory and helped patients receive treatment faster, with only those who test positive for malaria receiving medication."

Dr. Jacob Odipo, director of a health center in western Kenya

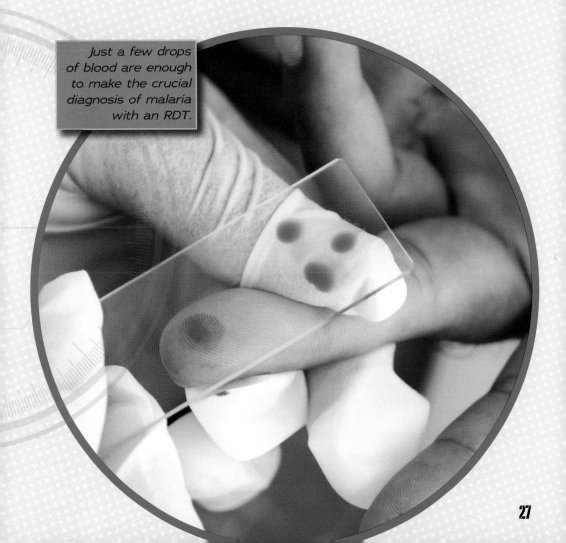

Just a few drops of blood are enough to make the crucial diagnosis of malaria with an RDT.

MEDICATION

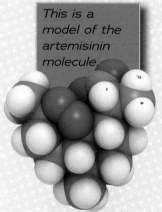

This is a model of the artemisinin molecule.

Once malaria is diagnosed, it must be treated quickly with drugs. For falciparum malaria, the most effective drugs are called artemisinin-based combination therapies (ACTs). Efforts to extend the distribution and use of ACTs are effective, but there are signs that the malaria parasite is now developing some resistance to the drugs.

ACTs

For centuries, the wormwood plant was used in China to treat malaria. When scientists investigated this, they identified the useful substance in the plant, artemisinin, and used it to develop antimalarial drugs. A full-course treatment for children costs $1 and cures them in one to three days. Treatment should start within 24 hours after the first symptoms occur. For vivax malaria, the drugs chloroquine and primaquine are given.

About 230 million doses of ACTs are needed every year and 19 million doses of vivax malaria treatment. Roll Back Malaria reports that, in 2010, more than 229 million ACTs were procured worldwide, up from only 2.1 million in 2003. Several companies and organizations, including the Medicines for Malaria Venture, are investing in ACTs to increase the breadth and depth of the supply of these vital drugs.

RESISTANT MOSQUITOES

In 2008, researchers found that malaria parasites in Cambodia were resistant to ACTs. The problem has since spread to other parts of Southeast Asia. In response, scientists have examined the genetic make-up of 800 malaria parasites from around the world and have found three distinct drug-resistant groups. If they can understand these genetic mutations, it will help them to quickly spot and track these strains if they spread farther.

"Malaria control efforts work and we know what to do. On artemisinin resistance, policymakers need to act quickly to avoid its spread or emergence in new areas."

Dr. Robert Newman, director of WHO Global Malaria Program

This floating village in Cambodia is very susceptible to malaria because it is so close to the lake's water. Malaria parasites are developing resistance to ACTs here.

AFFORDABLE TREATMENT

One of the challenges in getting malaria treatment to the people who need it is the fact that the drugs are often too expensive for local people to buy. Malaria-endemic countries tend to be flooded with supplies of cheaper drugs, called monotherapies, which do not work very well. Work is underway to address this problem.

RESEARCH AND DEVELOPMENT

Pharmaceutical research and development is expensive so the drugs produced are often costly to buy. Organizations, such as the Clinton Foundation in the United States, are committed to improving this situation. They work with the drug companies and the governments of developing countries to negotiate price reductions for drugs. They can also help to customize products for these poorer countries and improve the chains of supply so that the drugs reach the locations where they are needed most. The Clinton Foundation estimates that drug-pricing agreements have saved the developing world more than $1 billion and millions of lives.

It takes many scientists working for many years to develop new drugs to treat diseases such as malaria.

THE CASE OF ANGOLA

In Angola, in southwest Africa, a three-year program was set up in cooperation with the Ministry of Health to sell a subsidized ACT drug through private pharmacies. The aim was to increase the use of this quality-assured ACT, while reducing its price. At the start of the project, ACTs were $20–$40 per treatment. The price in the program was reduced to less than $1 per treatment. More than 1 million ACTs were distributed through the private pharmacies for the treatment of malaria in children under five years of age. Pharmacy staff was also trained in dispensing the drugs, and education activities in the surrounding communities were established. Sales data show an increase in the market share of ACTs from 4 percent in 2009 to 86 percent in 2011. At the same time, sales of the monotherapies declined dramatically.

On the Battlefield

The US Food and Drug Administration (FDA) is developing an innovative Counterfeit Detection Device, called CD-3. It hopes this handheld device will be able to identify fake or substandard antimalarial medicines quickly, preventing them from being sold and used for treatment.

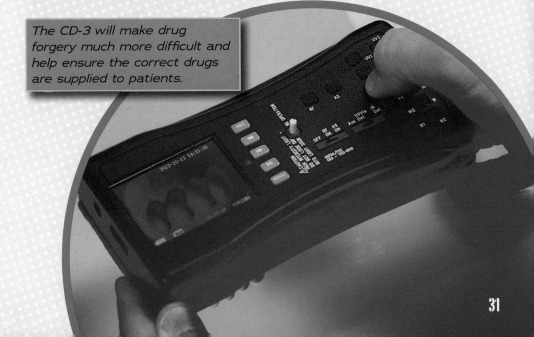

The CD-3 will make drug forgery much more difficult and help ensure the correct drugs are supplied to patients.

CHARITABLE EFFORT

The work of scientists, health professionals, and many others is often brought together and put into practice by nonprofit organizations. Under the umbrella of the Roll Back Malaria Partnership, the biggest nonprofit organization working against the disease, is Malaria No More. It works to raise not only awareness, but also funding.

malaria
NO MORE

Malaria No More works tirelessly to defeat malaria around the world.

MALARIA NO MORE

Malaria No More is based in New York with offices in the United Kingdom, Canada, and the Netherlands. The organization's mission is to end malaria deaths in Africa by involving world leaders, informing the public, and delivering lifesaving tools and education to families across Africa. Since 2006, the organization has protected almost 6 million people with mosquito nets and contributed to the 45 percent decline in deaths from malaria since 2000.

CLOSING THE GAP

Power of One is Malaria No More's campaign to engage the global public and the world's most innovative companies to help close the malaria testing and treatment gap in Africa using the latest mobile, social, and e-commerce technologies. Just one dollar donated to the campaign—via the website—will provide lifesaving screening and treatment for one child.

A US company that manufactures the innovative RDT, for example, has given 2 million testing kits to the Power of One project.

USING CELL PHONES

In another initiative, Malaria No More is highlighting the potential of technology to defeat malaria. Cell phones are increasingly being used in development projects worldwide. Malaria No More says cell phones can help accelerate progress toward malaria elimination. For example, health workers and researchers can use smartphones to collect data and upload it to online databases in real time. Also, in their NightWatch campaigns, they send text messages directly to families in Cameroon, Chad, Senegal, and Tanzania reminding them to use control measures such as nets.

"The benefits of integrating mobile technology into development research are making a tangible difference to the quality, speed, and effectiveness of fieldwork."

Malaria No More

Text messages sent by smartphones can remind people to use preventive measures such as mosquito nets treated with insecticide.

CHAPTER 5: GONE FOREVER

The elimination of malaria means reducing its spread to zero. This was once thought to be impossible, but today people are starting to talk about it as a real possibility. This is thanks to the huge global effort that has been made against the disease on many fronts.

These schoolchildren in Swaziland, Africa, are benefitting from their country's huge effort against malaria.

A THREE-STEP PROGRAM

In 2008, the Bill and Melinda Gates Foundation hosted "The Consultation on Research and Development for Malaria Eradication." This meeting engaged a group of experts across all areas of malaria interventions to develop a framework for considering the issues involved and to lay out a process to organize these efforts. It focused on three areas: improving vector control; improving supply and distribution of treatment drugs and developing new ones (especially that target the disease when the parasites are still multiplying in the liver); and the urgent development of vaccines. Drugs and vaccines need to target both kinds of malaria.

ELIMINATING MALARIA

The Clinton Foundation is helping Swaziland, a country in southern Africa, to advance toward becoming the first mainland African country to eliminate malaria. The foundation hopes to improve surveillance to track down and diagnose every case. Even a few years ago, people thought that eliminating malaria in a sub-Saharan African country was impossible, and yet Swaziland might now achieve that remarkable feat.

Roll Back Malaria has set a target of seeing significant progress toward elimination in at least eight to ten countries by 2015. Some people criticize this focus on the elimination of malaria. They say it diverts attention away from the more urgent need to deal with the severity of the disease today.

"Eradication of malaria is the only acceptable long-term goal. The costs will be substantial, but finite; the benefits immeasurable and lasting as savings in finance and human misery accumulate, the need to invest in the development of new drugs and vaccines wanes, and information systems and the supply chains are strengthened with benefits into the future."

David Schellenberg, professor of Malaria and International Health at the School of Hygiene and Tropical Medicine, London, England

An aggressive antimalaria program could mean that children in all African countries, such as these Kenyan children, never fall victim to malaria.

A Good Start

Since the start of the latest global push against malaria at the beginning of the new millennium, some excellent progress has been made. More than 20 countries with low levels of the disease, mainly in the Middle East, Eurasia, North Africa, and the Americas, are striving to eliminate it. As this happens, the costs of prevention and treatment fall drastically. The risk of malaria returning also declines.

A Decline in Deaths

Half of all the countries where malaria is endemic are on track to reduce cases by 75 percent by 2015. The global estimated incidence of malaria has decreased by 17 percent since 2000, and deaths have decreased by about 33 percent. That means that more than 1.1 million deaths from malaria have been prevented. In Southeast Asia, the number of malaria deaths has declined in six countries—Cambodia, Philippines, Lao People's Democratic Republic, Suriname, Thailand, and Vietnam. In the Americas, there are 22 malarial countries, with Brazil the worst affected. Cases in the Americas declined by

These children in Cambodia live in an area where the fight against malaria is achieving good levels of success.

30.5 percent between 2000 and 2007 as a result of better access to diagnosis and prevention, stronger health systems, and better early detection systems. Brazil's control program is still quite new, but, even in the first year, hospital admissions for malaria fell by one-third.

Three countries in the Americas have reached the elimination stage of combating the disease: Argentina, El Salvador, and Paraguay. Mexico has now reached the pre-elimination stage, with just a few remaining cases of malaria.

A FRAGILE STATE

The reduction in malaria cases and deaths is great news. However, as Dr. Rob Newman, director of the Global Malaria Program at WHO stated, these hard fought gains are fragile: "A decade of progress can be lost in a single malaria transmission season. Preventing the reintroduction of malaria is not just getting to the finish line, but once you're there making sure you're not knocked back." Sri Lanka, Zanzibar, and Swaziland are examples of places that have come tantalizingly close to ridding themselves of malaria but then faced rapid resurgences when efforts were not sustained. All are now back on track and working hard toward elimination.

In El Salvador, where these children live, malaria is on the point of being eliminated.

MALARIA IN AFRICA

Almost 700 million people in sub-Saharan Africa are at risk of contracting malaria. Although the region remains the worst hit for malaria, progress has been made. Eight African countries have reduced malaria by more than 50 percent since 2000. Africa has seen an amazing 33 percent decrease in malaria deaths since 2006.

QUICK PROGRESS

The results of the fight against malaria can be quick and dramatic. For example, in Rwanda, after giving out insecticidal mosquito nets and providing the right drug treatments to sick patients, malaria deaths among young children fell by 66 percent from 2005 to 2007. In Ethiopia in the same period, they fell by 51 percent. In 2013, Roll Back Malaria in South Africa issued a report on progress there from 2000 to 2012. In that period, cases of malaria and deaths from the disease both fell by more than 80 percent. However, national figures often hide wide variations within countries. Children living in urban areas and in developed regions are much more likely to sleep under nets than those living in rural or the poorest areas.

Mobile health clinics like this one in Rwanda have dramatically reduced the number of deaths from malaria.

ARTESUNATE

Africa has more cases of severe malaria than anywhere else. Very sick children who are having fits may not be able to take medication by mouth. They may also be too far from a medical facility to be given injections. Recent research has produced a new therapy to save lives in this critical situation. It is a drug called artesunate, which is given as a suppository. A single dose of artesunate can keep a child alive while he or she travels to a hospital to receive definitive treatment. It can be stored and given out by community leaders or village health workers.

Spraying more malarial areas, known as vector control, has also reduced levels of the disease.

On the Battlefield

The Special Programme for Research and Training in Tropical Diseases (TDR) is a global program of scientific collaboration that helps facilitate, support, and influence efforts to combat diseases of poverty. It funded clinical trials of artesunate in Bangladesh, Ghana, and Tanzania over two years. The results were very encouraging. The trials have also helped the development of research centers in the countries involved.

CHAPTER 6: THE FUTURE

The past decade has seen a massive global effort against malaria, with some excellent results. The challenge for the future is to keep up the pressure against this disease to advance the science and the work on the ground to push toward its elimination.

PRIORITIES

Twenty-five countries are on track to eliminate malaria altogether in the not too distant future. This has been possible because of a massive increase in international funding for the fight against malaria since 2000. There are two priorities for the future. The first is to improve the distribution and use of the tools already available. These include preventive measures such as mosquito nets, vector control, and treatment during pregnancy, as well as diagnostic and treatment options. The second is to push the boundaries of research to find new preventive measures and treatments. These are vital because of the malaria parasite's ability to develop resistance to the insecticides and drugs developed so far.

Increasing the distribution of current antimalarial treatments will help control the disease while more effective drugs are being tested for future use.

Drug companies are putting huge resources into finding new malaria drugs.

Developing Drugs

The fight against drug resistance is being fought in laboratories around the world. One solution is to develop drugs that can be taken in a single dose each day rather than in a complicated pattern. This makes it more likely that patients will take them properly, get well, then stop taking them. Prolonged inefficient use gives the parasite more chance to develop resistance. New drugs are also needed. Five new drugs for late-stage malaria are in development, as well as a radical new drug for vivax malaria. New, nonartemisinin combination drugs are needed. Experts say that ideally a radically new treatment should be launched every five years.

"The malaria community is set to do all it takes over the next five years to ensure that malaria medicines reach those who need them most. We are still challenged by lack of universal access to rapid tests and treatments, and by the possibility that resistance could spread. MMV has in its pipeline compounds that will help counter resistance, and we are doing everything in our power to accelerate the development of these compounds into malaria medicines."

Dr. David Reddy,
CEO of Medicines for
Malaria Venture

A Malaria Vaccine?

Vaccination has been shown to be the most effective single weapon in the fight against many serious infectious diseases, such as measles and polio. It protects people from catching the disease. As yet there is no vaccine for malaria, but a huge amount of work is being done to develop one.

Malaria Vaccine Technology Roadmap Process

From 2005 to 2006, more than 230 experts representing 100 organizations participated in a collaboration called the Malaria Vaccine Technology Roadmap Process. Its goals were by 2015 to develop a falciparum malaria vaccine with a protective efficacy of more than 50 percent and which lasts longer than one year. By 2025, it hoped to develop one with a protective efficacy of more than 80 percent and which lasts longer than four years. There are significant challenges in this work. No vaccine has ever been developed against a parasite —they all target bacteria or viruses. The malaria parasite is extremely complex, so scientists are trying to unlock its genetic makeup.

This is an image of the malaria plasmodium in the placenta of an infected mother. The disease is still a deadly threat to mothers and their unborn babies.

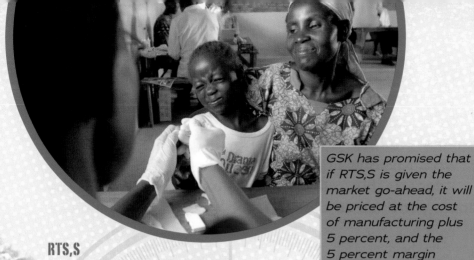

RTS,S

British drug company GlaxoSmithKline (GSK) has been working on a malaria vaccine for three decades. In 2013, the company announced the results of the trials of a malaria vaccine known as RTS,S. They tested the vaccine in Africa's largest-ever clinical trial, involving almost 15,500 children in seven countries. The results showed that the vaccine almost halved the number of malaria cases in young children and reduced by around one-quarter the number of malaria cases in infants. WHO has indicated it may recommend use of the RTS,S vaccine as early as 2015 if it receives a license from the necessary regulatory bodies.

GSK has promised that if RTS,S is given the market go-ahead, it will be priced at the cost of manufacturing plus 5 percent, and the 5 percent margin will be reinvested in malaria research.

"Given the huge disease burden of malaria among African children, we cannot ignore what these latest results tell us about the potential for RTS,S to have a measurable and significant impact on the health of millions of young children in Africa."

David Kaslow, vice president of product development at PATH

Can We Win the War?

The successes that have been gained in the battle against malaria show that this is a war that can be won. Millions of lives have been saved in the past decade, but millions more have been lost. Many people continue to die from this devastating disease.

A Global Commitment

People all over the world are committed to fighting malaria. Some of them work in laboratories, researching vaccines, drugs, and medical techniques. Some work in governments and positions of authority, where their influence can make change happen. Others are working on the ground, helping people in the community. They may be health professionals, educators, or charity workers. To enable the work of all these people to continue, they must be constantly seeking innovative ways forward.

Investment is needed to ensure malaria is eradicated in communities still devastated by the disease.

Malaria and Money

Billions of dollars have been spent on the fight against malaria in the last decade. Now that the MDG for 2015 is approaching, Roll Back Malaria is seeking a commitment from donors of all kinds that they will continue to give. The greatest threat to malaria control in the short term does not come from the development of resistance by the parasite, but from the lack of resources. Roll Back Malaria estimates that $5 billion is needed each year but so far only $2.3 billion is being made available. It is clear that donor support will continue to be needed for the foreseeable future. It is simply unacceptable that today a child dies every minute from a disease that can be controlled because of a lack of a $3 mosquito net, a 50-cent diagnostic test, or a 40-cent treatment.

BEATING MALARIA, BEATING POVERTY

Combating malaria means so much more than simply keeping people well or curing the sick. People who are well can go to school and to work. They can earn money and build futures for themselves and their families. If successful, the global war being waged against the microscopic malaria parasite is one that will change lives everywhere.

"The global campaign against malaria has shown what is possible when the international community joins forces on multiple fronts to tackle a disease that takes its heaviest toll on poor and underprivileged populations ... The advances of recent years show that the battle against malaria can be won."

**UN Secretary General
Ban Ki-moon**

International politicians and organization leaders, including UN Secretary General Ban Ki-moon, are now spearheading the drive to eliminate malaria.

GLOSSARY

BACTERIUM a single-celled living pathogen that can cause disease

CHLOROQUINE a drug used to protect against malaria

CONTRACTING developing a disease

CUSTOMIZE to adapt something specifically for a customer or personal preference

EPIDEMIC a fast-spreading disease

ERADICATE to destroy or completely get rid of something

INNOVATIONS new things or ways of doing something

INSECTICIDE a chemical that kills insects

LARVICIDE a chemical that kills insect larvae

MALARIA an infectious disease caused by the parasite plasmodium

MONOTHERAPY a single drug used as a treatment for disease

PALUDRINE a drug used against malaria

PANDEMIC an epidemic that has spread worldwide

PATHOGENS microorganisms that cause disease

PLASMODIUM the parasite that causes malaria

PROTOZOON a parasite, a single-celled living pathogen that can cause disease

SHELF LIFE the length of time that a drug remains effective after its manufacturing

STILLBIRTHS the births of babies that have died inside the uterus

VACCINATION giving the body a weakened version of a disease so that the immune system can build up resistance to it

VACCINE a weakened version of a disease which is given to people to protect them from the full-blown version

VECTOR CONTROL the killing of disease-causing animals

VIRUS a nonliving pathogen that causes disease when it invades the body

For More Information

Books

Goldsmith, Connie. *Dangerous Infectious Diseases* (Invisible Invaders). New York, NY: Twenty First Century Books, 2006.

Ollhof, Jim. *Malaria* (A History of Germs). Minneapolis, MN: ABDO & Daughters, 2009.

Person, Stephen. *Malaria: Super Killer!* (Nightmare Plagues). New York, NY: Bearport Publishing, 2010.

Websites

Find out about malaria at:
eschooltoday.com/malaria/malaria-facts-and-tips-for-kids.html

Discover more about Malaria No More's campaign Power of One at:
www.po1.org

Find out about World Malaria Day at:
www.rollbackmalaria.org/worldmalariaday/index.html

INDEX